holiday in the islands of grief

pitt poetry series ed ochester, editor

holiday in the islands of grief

jeffrey mcdaniel

university of pittsburgh press

Published by the University of Pittsburgh Press, Pittsburgh, Pa., 15260

Copyright © 2020, Jeffrey McDaniel

All rights reserved

Manufactured in the United States of America

Printed on acid-free paper

10 9 8 7 6 5 4 3 2 1

ISBN 13: 978-0-8229-6610-4

ISBN 10: 0-8229-6610-7

Cover painting: Jasmin Siddiqui (aka Hera from Herakut).

Cover design: Joel W. Coggins

In Memoriam

Drew O'Leary (1968–2012)
David Morrison (1953–2013)
Thomas Lux (1946–2017)
Walter McDaniel (1938–2017)
Jamie Ricks (1963–2017)
Creigh Horvath (1968–2019)

contents

Before

2017

November

holiday in the islands of grief

Before

Hearing Test

"Headlight." The word so faint,
its consonants: a lucent flicker
in sonic darkness. I seal my lids.
"Cut" she says. Or was it *cup*? "Cut,"
I repeat back. I'm pressed against
the glass cliff of fifty. In a sound booth
not recording a rap song, or being interviewed
by Terry Gross. I'm being tested
to see how much sound flitters
like sand through the colander
of my ears. "Cupcake." The next word
so quiet, I clench. That feeling of knowing
she's said something, but unsure
what it is. That place between silence
and what you're able to hear. Like being a child
and watching your parents whisper
on the other side of the room. Except
you're not a child. Your hair is vanishing
like a glacier. Your left knee is officially
a bum begging for change on the basketball court.
The expanding clump of steel wool
in your lungs making you gasp
in cold rooms. The disassembling
has begun. That point when the doctor
stops saying he can make you better.
You're an old banged up car in Cuba. Your teeth
keep breaking on pieces of candy. "Sunlight"
she says, and you raise your hand, the new signal
to let her know you hear. And your face tightens
as you wonder if this is what it will feel like:
total darkness and 99% silence, a cramped
contained space, the faint sound

of someone talking nearby, but you can't
make out the words, and you wonder
who's standing up there, arranging flowers
or drinking wine. Or maybe it's just a jogger.
Or the sound of your daughter's voice,
the one thing you want to take with you,
the weight of her lying flat on your stomach
at three, saying "sandwich," your palm
wedged into the crib for her head to lay on
at two. "Hand pillow." The adobe smell
of her hair. How her cuddled into your chest
is the closest you've ever felt to home.

"Gigantic"

I'm transcribing a second-grade creative writing exercise
when I realize I have been misspelling *penguin* my whole life.

Bands are said to be selling out when a song appears
in a commercial, but don't the Pixies get a pass

for "Gigantic"? Don't they deserve a little icing
off the cake they built? Crap—that's a mixed metaphor,

and it doesn't make sense. *Sense is overrated*
says the dance therapist in my brain. *Watch out*

for your bruised ribs says the mother in my solar plexus.
I'll only see the nurse, if you get me more Xanax says my mother

in real life. Twenty years ago, I met a French girl
in a gigantic nightclub in Prague. Plopped on stage,

chin propped on hands—if you drew a cartoon of a sad girl
in a club, it would be her. Some guy had just dumped her.

A friend drove her to Prague on a cheer-you-up road trip.
The fiction writer in my head says *this would be a great place*

to add some tactile details, if you want to make this engaging
for a general reader, but I don't want to talk about how the club,

Repre, was the size of a gymnasium in the basement
of the Czech version of Carnegie Hall, with a lunette mosaic

in the lobby and a marble staircase. I don't feel like talking
about how the bandana-wearing DJ was on a scaffold

and unleashed "Killing in the Name of," and the Euros started moshing,
and their mosh pits were genetically more gentle

than American mosh pits. Anyway, the next night at dawn
Delphine, the French girl, said the Pixies were the only good thing

that had come from America, and we did that thing
where you make fun of each other's country, overlooking the Vlatva,

gushing under Charles Bridge, with its gauntlet of holy statues,
the sky an orange dream over Prague Castle.

I was so stupid when it came to women. My pride
got wounded, and my hackles went up. And what the fuck

are *hackles*, and now it's twenty years later—again it's five a.m.,
and the sun is mutilating coke parties up and down the eastern seaboard,

and I'm middle-aged, and just learned *penguin* isn't spelled with a *q*,
thinking of Delphine and crossing Charles Bridge at dawn,

the struck-match sun ricocheting off the silver on her fingers, the stone
saints and I all enamored with the mercury in her eyes.

Midlife Chrysler

You're on a used car lot. The wind blows
through what's left of your hair like high school boy breath

through a cheerleader's skirt. *Sale Discount Sale*
wiggles in the wind. You have ten thousand dollars cash

in one pocket and a bottle of Viagara in the other.
"Want to hop in the saddle?" the saleswoman asks,

tapping the hood of a beige Chrysler. Her smile is a slice
of red velvet cake being snuck into a church. Her shawl says

with the lights out. Her black leather boots say
with the lights on. The road opens up like the mouth

of the first girl you ever kissed, in a grimy alley
behind a Philly arcade. She grabs the stereo knob,

cranks up the soundtrack of your life. Until this moment
you swore you were Bauhaus, but the speakers pour out Journey,

that watered-down bourbon of a rock band. You grip the wheel
and glide through a yellow light. A cop stands on the corner

juggling hand grenades like a robot's genitalia. *Ok,* you say,
your eyelids dropping like coins from the palm of a beggar.

Bio from a Parallel World

Jeffrey McDaniel lives in a small apartment
in Philadelphia. His hair gathered back

into a ponytail. His smile: a wobbly
merry-go-round that he hopes you will get on.

He treads water in the same dive bar
every Thursday night. He smiles at each girl

who stumbles in and says: W*ould you like to ride
the Tilt-a-Whirl?* Notice how each one of his teeth

is a different shade of yellow. Then he flutters
into the bathroom and digs a rollercoaster

out of his pocket. Jeffrey McDaniel inherited
a lot of breadsticks when he was twelve

from his dead grandfather. He has a fake shrine
in his backyard. Sometimes his brothers call him

and ask to borrow lawn furniture. In his pocket,
the calls go staight to voicemail: *Hi there,*

you sexy little dumpling. Welcome to my earlobe.
Please breathe hard into the mouthpiece. Jeffrey McDaniel

runs his hands along the two *f*s in his name
like elephant tusks and shakes his head like a bucket

full of soggy trademarks, then he stomps out
of the bathroom and finds a pool of bourbon

hovering near his stool. Girls he knew in college
lounge in bathing suits. He yanks off his t-shirt,

struts out onto the diving board, and cannonballs
into his future, which smells just like his past.

The Bottom of My Hourglass

I'm so bored I can literally hear each grain of sand
splat on the pile of time at the bottom of my hourglass.

My twelve-year-old daughter has just told me
to go fuck myself and locked herself in a Porta Potty

in a minor league baseball parking lot. I see my therapist's smug face
in the clouds. I want to kick this moveable lavatory,

but someone's got to be the grown-up. "James?" I turn—
a high school romance holds cotton candy, her eyes

the same blue whispers flashing glimmers from her head.
No ring on her finger. No sin in her singular. Pleasantries

exchanged. Smiles enunciated. The teeth that hickeyed me up
in the back of Peter Maschal's van on prom night

are still Easter Sunday white. I can feel the Jesus in the cave
of my Calvin's stir back to life. *Forgive me Father,*

for I have singed my fingertips on the waist of a woman
with microwave hips in the back of a Buick, and then my daughter

steps out of the Porta Potty, and she's in a white dress,
garlands in her hair, violins drawing a moustache

on the face of eternity, and she grabs me by the elbow,
and I walk her down the aisle strewn with petals and subway tokens.

Pass the Gravy

It's one of those days
when the cold opens
it's off-white mouth and nibbles
your gloveless fingers,
with its tiny lacerating teeth,
then ascends to that inch
of exposed skin
between your hat's brim
and your jacket collar
and drags its champagne
bucket tongue. Then slithers
its frosty yardstick
of a finger up your pant leg
and rubs freezer burn
on your calves. Be thankful
the train will be here
any minute, you think,
bouncing between boots
on the platform when
the announcer coughs
out a delay, and the stiff wind,
which is the cold's laughter,
lashes your cheeks,
like being smacked
with a wet dish rag
at a family dinner.

The Appraiser

The day started like any other: a VW Bug
with a deer-crunched fender, followed by a flipped Volvo

flat-bedded back from the desert, then a two-Heineken lunch
and a RAV 4 with dings on three panels. There was some pot

in the happy hour parking lot, a sunset that looked like
listening to Joy Division in a bathtub, as a trio of birds

circled the pink sky like a dog chopped into parts,
Damien Hirst–style, but still alive and chasing its tail.

Back in the bar, I overheard a snippet of a couple's argument,
and was lit just enough to stick my snout in and tell them

who was at fault. You see a car on its side and blood
on the pavement. I see the penmanship of the Lord,

the seeds of negligence in the drip, drip of an oil leak.
A mere glance at a skid mark and I can hear the brakes howl,

feel the car's left wheels rising from the pavement,
a stream of vowels spurting from the sunroof's mouth.

My Adobe Bouquet

Each winter, we sit around the Mexican lagoon, like Persephone
and Hades, sipping cocktails as crocodiles slink through swamp water,

shards of constellations, visible through palm trees.
I can almost forget her other lovers, but then she smiles

a little too wide, and I think of all the men that have soaked
in her mouth's natural hot spring—*enough to fill the lagoon*

she once joked, and the bones in my shoulders crumble.
I just want to do something with her in the dark she's never done.

So I stand exactly a foot behind her and let the wind bring me
scoops of her scent as the howler monkeys go la-la in the trees.

I step forward an inch each minute, till our bodies are pressed together
like the pages of a banned book. And that's enough for me—

but then the moon opens its big fat mouth and shines a floodlight
into the lagoon, and all the men she's been with are illuminated,

and I see the drummer's hairy back, the chiseled jaws of the twins,
the butcher's fat fingers, and I slide to her feet, like a dress

she's stepping out of. And now she's fifty-feet tall:
a cigarette in one hand and a warrant for my arrest in the other.

She laughs, revealing a mouthful of crocodile teeth, and the cicadas
sing louder, like the wheels of Satan's chariot in the distance.

The Price of History

You're at a bus stop, wool hat
tugged down. Slush sprays

up from the tires of a bus
wheezing to a halt. You lumber onboard

and smell the nachos and beer breath
of the man who peers into the crevice

of your mostly zipped-up jacket.
You close your eyes and remember

being fifteen, your parents' Baltimore
rooftop, the sun blaring down

like a golden trumpet. You stripped
to sunbathe on the asphalt

with three friends, the smokestacks
clearing their throats over the oak trees.

The face of Darius, the one black kid
in your class, froze as you lifted

your t-shirt and revealed
a Confederate flag one-piece

that you thought was a Union Jack
when you bought it on sale

at a mall in Virginia. *Want to get high,*
you asked in a British accent,

as his smile fled like smoke
from the pinched wick of a candle.

The Church of Michael Jordan

The hoop is not metal, but a pair of outstretched arms,
God's arms, joined at the fingers. And God is saying

throw it to me. It's not a ball anymore. It's an orange prayer
I'm offering with all four chambers. And the other players—

the Pollack of limbs, flashing hands and teeth—
are just temptations, obstacles between me and the Lord's light.

Once during an interview, I slipped, *I didn't pray well tonight,*
and the reporter looked at me, the same one who'd called me

"a player of destiny," and said *you mean "play," right*? Of course,
I nodded. Priests embarrass me. A real priest

wouldn't put on that robe. A real priest works in disguise,
leads by example, preaches with his feet. Yes, Jesus walked on water,

but how about a staircase of air? When the clock
is down to its final ticks, I rise, and over the palms

of a nonbeliever—the whole world watching, thinking
it can't be done—I let the faith roll off my fingers, the ball

giddy with backspin, an arena of people clutching
the same breath, the ball hanging in the air like a question,

then the net's curtain flying up, the Lord's truth visible
for an instant and everyone swearing *miracle.*

The Imperial Diet

for Barack Obama

You can enjoy it for breakfast
with a couple slices of salmon and egg whites
staring up at you from the plate.

You can straw-drink it ice blended with raspberries
and yogurt and a dash of spinach
after a vigorous session of hopscotch.

You can swig it for lunch with two open-faced burgers
the size of palms fresh off the grill.

You can pound it on national television
in one patriotic gulp, as congressmen chant
chug, chug, chug, chug.

You can down it with pork chops in an opaque glass
just after leading your children in prayer.

You can attack it with a spoon for dessert in a porcelain bowl
with a nose of whipped cream on top.

You can toss it back as a nightcap
with celery and pitted olives and Tabasco sauce
as the fireplace crackles
thin wooden arms into flames

You can midnight duck into a closet and force it down
after making love with your wife.

You can say *cheers,* or *to security,* or *honor,*
or *farm to table,* or *too much salt,* or *goddamn you, America.*

You can wince. You can cry. You can curse
your own face in the mirror,
but you will drink it, Mr. President,
your daily glass of blood.

Good Boy Now

Mom, I know I was never your favorite,
but I will be good now
and spray you with perfume
that smells like a boy
who set his arm hairs on fire.
I'll be good now. I'll sit out here
all night, lighting matches,
thinking of a firefly fluttering
through your cave-dark veins.
Remember when you said
the nine months you carried me
was like having your worst enemy
live inside you? I wish Santa
had filled your uterus with coal.
I want to live beside you now, mom.
I've got a tent I can pitch by your tombstone.
I'll stare at the moon, like a dried womb
in the sky. I'll light matches
and remember the thimble of gasoline
I poured onto your dress in the casket.

Raymond

It was rumored that as a three-year-old
his mother dropped him on his psyche
making it surrender its illusion of unity.

Imagine the offspring of a cherub
and a cracked windshield
and you get the gist.

Imagine yellow shoelaces enhancing
the oceanic green of his eyes.

He was the burned-out bulb
behind the *x* in *Exit,*
the electrical cord insinuating
what a good noose it would be.

That slink in his smile, that fishhook
tugging on his upper right lip,
which even in photographs provided
a hint of motion, as if some raven
was luring him up to the sky.

Jonathan

We are underwater off the coast of Belize.
The water is lit up even though it's dark
as if there are illuminated seashells
scattered on the ocean floor.
We're not wearing oxygen tanks,
yet staying underwater for long stretches.
We are looking for the body of the boy
we lost. Each year he grows a little older.
Last December I opened his knapsack
and stuck in a plastic box of carrots.
Even though we're underwater, we hear
a song playing over a policeman's radio.
He comes to the shoreline to park
and eat midnight sandwiches, his headlights
fanning out across the harbor.
And I hold you close, apple of my closed eye,
red dance of my opened fist.

Dear Drew

There's a green leaf stuck to my window. The red veins,
when hit by the sun, look like your arms

the morning they found you sprawled on your futon,
like the astronaut who didn't get to go. Now you're rising

out of your body, like steam from a kettle. You used to say
there ought to be red bloodlines in money, so we'd remember

all the pain it took to make. A blue-sealed baggie
at your feet, sprinkles of moon dust in your mustache.

Remember how we hid in my closet in first grade,
a place our glazed and lipsticked mothers couldn't reach?

At fifteen, we smoked the dust of angels
to form an atmospheric barrier their meteors

couldn't breach. I can see you now in your rocket-shaped
coffin, wearing an astronaut suit over pajamas

with little race cars on the sleeves. All the cops
and taxi drivers who chased us. All the lies we told.

All the men we asked to buy us quarts of beer
outside of delis. All the doormen we scored weed from.

All the battles on asphalt. All the lines
of blow we inhaled like gunpowder

igniting sticks of dynamite in our brains. At twenty, taking
my dad's car to Florida on a whim. At twelve, scrawling

Manning Street Boys in black marker under the top mattress
of your bunk bed. Wincing-down whisky and comparing

preteen dicks in your basement. Our Irish Catholic mothers
with their seashells of wine and perfume. The prettiest moms

in Center City. All the Thanksgivings together.
That time we watched your older sister through the wooden slats

of an outdoor shower at the shore, her puff of hair
so much realer than anything we saw in my father's *Playboys*.

The time you passed out under a pinball machine at Wizards
and woke with your jeans shimmed down your hips.

How at sixteen you'd introduce me to girls on South Street
and whisper: "He's a little weird. He writes poems."

And how twenty-five years later you'd call me up
barreling through the night's tunnel with a payload fairing in your veins

and read my poems back to me. How you showed up
at my mom's when her spine was dissolving and shouldered

her sofa down the stairs. How I heaved in a hotel on Broad Street,
hours before delivering your eulogy, the same street

where you marched as a Mummer. A mile away
from where we went to nursery school. Those Sears catalogues

you modeled in as a child. I wish you'd three a.m. wake me now
to dissect lines I've written in your drunken purr. I wish

I could hear your guillotine laugh, as you strutted
through Rittenhouse Square, where you held court at seventeen,

the iron goat we climbed on at three, as our mothers smiled
behind patterned scarves. I wish I could see you rising

for a jump shot and releasing it over the burnt fingertips
of a Two-Streeter, while kids from Shot Tower yelled *next*.

I wish I could see you rise past the seventeenth-floor window
at the Dorchester where we hurled a milk carton and watched

a windshield shatter with a loud, echo-y pop. But all I see is the sun
dripping out sour light like a squeezed lemon. At the church podium,

I told the story of us chased down the alley by that cab driver,
whose car we hit with eggs. How you, trapped behind me,

kept saying *Hurry up, Jeff,* your footsteps so close, your breath
brushing my neck, and when I got out of the alley, I turned

and you were gone. Afterward your divorced parents
told me separately what a good job I'd done,

how I'm so brilliant and you're so dead, stuck
in detention in the underworld. No one ever looked up to me

the way you did. For months, I called your number,
just to hear your voice on the outgoing message,

but then some random jackass answered and said *what the fuck,*
a response you surely would've laughed at.

2017

Destruction Myth

There was a supersonic creak and then the sun
plummeted, leaving a streak of yellow
smeared on the sky's blue wall. A large rusty nail
covered in blood, where the sun used to be.

The next day, the trees flapped
their green branches in unison
and one by one they erupted
from the soil and flew across the blue
in the direction of the sun's departure.

The next day, you guessed it:
the birds said *fuck this shit* and flapped
their way out of the galaxy.

And then it got very dark.
The flashlights lasted a couple weeks.
The candles a few months more.
And then the world was as gloomy as the inside
of an accountant's ass. And the stars
glittered like stolen diamonds
spilled on a black velvet blanket.

And there was no more music.
except for the wind, combing its fingers
through the bald forest, wondering
where its hair had gone.

Holiday in the Islands of Grief

Here is your spit of sand, your own private tent
stitched together from your father's
Brooks Brothers shirts, a lock of his rust-colored hair
attached to the netting's zipper. Yes, the wind
cuts through it, but it's yours, and the sand
is always cool when you lie down upon it,
which is not often. Most of the time you're looking
out over the waves, trying to identify that line
where water meets sky. The first day you thought
every plane's vapor trail was his spirit leaving his body
and jetting skyward. Some nights you barefoot the shoreline
and wish you could call him—the Brillo of his voice
would feel like silk, but all you have is the voicemail
he left three weeks before the wind
was sucked out of his body with a tiny emerald straw.

You're not sure how long you will live here,
with this wind, howling through your pores,
eating whatever scaly creature washes up on the shore.
In the distance, you see other tents, see the bodies
of strangers heaving, but you can't hear their sobs,
and you won't offer condolences. It's dark
twenty-two hours each day. The other two
you sit in your cloth palace
because the sun's boiled light could scissor
your skin like Christmas paper. The worst
are the people whose loved ones almost pass.
They come halfway down the hillside with their backpacks
and bottles of water, and just like that
get called back to the living. On the day he died,
the sky was the same blue of his eye,

watered-down cerulean you're tempted
to call it, but then the wind comes
and puts all the broken pieces of silence
back into place.

Set Design Notes for a Seizure

Take a sibling, any sibling.
Place the sibling in a room.
Make him close to fifty.
Put furniture in the room.
An ashtray with fifty-seven butts.
A thick layer of dust on the closed blinds.
Like the blinds are wearing cheap makeup
       that has not been washed off in years.
A TV on in the background.
A bong on the table, next to his dead father's will.
High-powered prescription medicine bottles on the nightstand
like miniature silos.
Scatter seven half-finished Sprite cans around a desk.
Place piles of dirty clothes in the corners.
Make one of the prescription bottles empty. Empty for days.
Tease up one strand of hair in the center of his skull
       so it looks like a fuse.
Let's recognize that the terror in the sibling's eyes is real
       even as we acknowledge that the wind
       is coming from his own mind.
Let's acknowledge that there is a miniaturized duplicate version
       of the sibling inside his own body.
Let's see the sibling three a.m. careen down the apartment building
       hallway, his body gonging into metal doors.
Let's see a neighbor in his striped boxers step out.
Let's see the sibling's arms and long fingers start to shake
       like his toe is lodged in some invisible socket.
Let's see the sibling's head collide with the wall
       as he spirals to the carpet.
Let's see the neighbor's face as he dials 911.
Let's see the sibling's mouth foam up like an overpriced latte.
Let's see other neighbors peer out their apartment doors.

Let's watch the sibling stop shaking, like a wind-up toy
        that's run out of juice.
Let's hear the jackhammer footsteps of the ambulance people
        shuttling down the hallway.
Let's stay with the resuscitation audio
        and video cut to the sibling at seven years old.
Snapshots of him smiling in the fortress of his father's arms.
A cop's muffled speech in the background.
The audio of the sibling loaded onto a gurney,
as the fortress of his father's arms dissolves.

Bagpipes

I remember five half-drunk Diet Coke cans
plopped on the base of a bronze statue
about the Holocaust by a Polish sculptor.

I remember smudges of blood
on a half-buttoned dress shirt.
A pair of glasses swallowed
somewhere in the room's physical noise,
which was like the sea on a windy day,
frozen mid-crash.

I remember a rusty metal shopping cart
parked by the apartment door
packed with empty soda cans
and downed energy drinks
and my brother's Dos Equus bottles.

I remember ten thousand dollars' worth
of silver coins in a torn green trash bag.

I remember the lemony scent of urine
radiating outward from his rumpled throne,
like a lighthouse whispering, *beware,
beware, beware.*

The oxygen tank in the background.
A thick layer of dust on a pair
of brown leather penny loafers by the door.

I remember ten dress shirts at the local dry cleaner
that never got picked up. Three weeks of mail
stacked up on a pile of newspapers.

I remember reading *Gabriel* by Ed Hirsch
in the same café where I'm typing this now.

I remember the uneaten plates of food
once he moved into the home.

I remember him shrinking like a t-shirt
that kept getting washed.

I remember the invisible
clock ticking.

I remember instructing my daughter
to press handfuls of her dark hair to his nose.

I remember his right eye,
the only part of him that still moved,
the animated blue of his eye.

I remember his hand in mine,
and I rubbed my other hand
over the prairie stubble of his chest.

I remember the last scraps of breath
being tugged out.

I remember how when I entered the funeral parlor
I knew the body was no longer his. The way his lips
looked like they'd been sealed with glue.

I remember listening to the pastor and thinking
she never knew him.

I remember I was on the right side of the room.

I remember standing to read the eulogy
and my head filling with cotton.

I remember being certain he could hear me.

I remember my daughter sliding
a note into his pocket.

I remember my chest feeling like a rug on fire
being stamped out.

I remember the warm hand
of his college roommate.

I remember not wanting the lid to close.

I remember the man who ran the place
standing beside me and saying
he lost his father the year before,
which was his way of saying it was time to go.

I remember only bits of the bagpipe player
at the grave site. The cars whipping by
on the highway below.

I remember time was moving too fast
and there were only four of us
to shoulder the casket onto the pulley device
that would lower him into the dirt,

where he would take out my daughter's note
and read it in his voice of Bombay gin mixed with gravel.

Def Leppard

I'm delivering a eulogy tomorrow
and I need a root canal,
but there's a bigger plan.

The flesh has a way of becoming
resilient when adrenaline
gushes through your pulmonary factory.

The train is rocking
but not like Def Leppard.

The September sun casts shadows
shaped like sheep on a green hill.

The conductor comes and there is that panic
of touching the pocket and wondering
where the ticket went.

Fifty years of being disorganized will do that to you.

When I was twelve, I went to see Ted Nugent
at the Spectrum. He did that swinging out on a rope thing,
wearing a loin cloth. He did not announce himself
as a right-wing nutjob.

A few years ago, the deceased and I struggled
to remember who opened for Nugent.

The sky is a blue pasture dotted with sheep.

There are people in the clouds with ray guns.

The world is filled with dragons
and then we bang on the neighbor's door
in the middle of the night and our tongue
comes out like a doll's tongue and we can't speak
and our limbs are frozen and we start to chomp
on our tongue over and over
like it's the plug connecting us
to some invisible socket and our bodies
shake like we're being electrocuted,
like there's this glitch in the system
and we're suddenly revealed to be machines.
And then we go dark and the apartment building
neighbor calls 911 and the police come
and the ambulance and they load us
onto a stretcher and take us
back to the factory, but not before
walking into our door-wide-open apartment,
looking for our keys and instead finding
our weed and our bong, and all this because
we went rogue on the Ativan.

Everyone on this train is crying inside.

A thousand miles south of here
the wind is making the trees shake
like a stadium full of people
all having seizures simultaneously.

Rock and roll wants to make us
have slow-motion seizures. Rock and roll
wants us to use our tongues.

Watch the gap says the recorded voice
over the loudspeaker.

You can feel the threads holding you together
start to fray. Another tooth
began to die last week. The halogen bulb
in your hybrid car just burned out.

Tomorrow a room full of people will look to you
to make sense of why their friend
or father or relative was gunned down
at one a.m. on a Philly sidewalk,
and all you want to tell them
is how much pain there is in the world,
but you know there's a bigger plan
as you cradle the penicillin bottle,
you just can't remember what it is.

Yankees Playoff Game

Yes, the pitcher, Tanaka, is Japanese, and yes,
most of the fans have skin somewhere between

Elmer's glue and olive, and yes, I am beige
speckled with freckles, and yes, I love

this country, and yes, I'm standing.
And yes, if the flag can handle nearly a million

confederate soldiers jumping up and down
on the stars and stripes like a Kevlar trampoline,

then surely it can endure a few kneeling football players
with skin somewhere between the color of a whip

and the planks of a slave ship. Racism runs deep
like the 4 train under this stadium, deep

like the place Tanaka has to dig with a man on third
and one out, in a zero–zero elimination game, uncorking

a slider that starts high before plunging
to the dirt, the batter pulverizing only air. The slider:

a pitch whose father is a fastball and whose mother
is a curve. Last week a soccer mom from SUNY Maritime,

must have loved America a whole lot—after a college game
she yelled: "your girls kneeling is defiling the flag,

and this field doesn't even have a flag," and a man
I work with said "it's not about the flag, ma'am,

it's police brutality," and that's when it came out,
in 2017, in New York, from a mother, to a grown man's face,

"go back to Africa," and in that moment we see
how her patriotism and her racism had coiled

around each other so tightly one could no longer tell
where one ended and the other began. And last week

a 7th grade boy in my town was called a _____
by an 8th grade boy, and it turned out later

that the 8th grade boy was biracial too. America,
the plot is thickening. It's not pigment that binds us.

The paper the Constitution is printed on is white,
but the ink is black, America. My daughter's skin

is somewhere between a heater and a change-up.
America, do you want the good news

or the news that will make you quiver like an aluminum bat
at the Little League World Series? America,

do you want mustard or me to squeeze the last drops
of blood from a bald eagle onto this jive turkey burger? America,

the fans are on their feet, roaring for Tanaka,
as he paints his initials on the outside corner of the plate

in Japanese calligraphy. And now the Yankees
are batting, America, and even with eyes closed one can feel

the solid bat crack swallowed by the fan gasp, swelling
into an ocean wave of glee as the ball lifts and lifts

and clears the fence. And then the 7th inning stretch,
an opera singer belting out God Bless, you, America,

and tears grow thick in my eyes. Is it love of you
or the Jumbo Cam scanning the wrinkled tablecloth

of an eighty-year-old veteran's face?

St. Pat's

On Metro North, city-bound, the Hudson
unspooling. *The surface is glassy and then sometimes*

it ripples, says my ten-year-old, Camilla,
as if she's describing the python-like body of Time

slithering through our fingers. We get a text:
Julia, her basketball-playing babysitter, needs

ligament surgery. The train releases us
from its long, thin body. Three years from now,

Camilla, in puberty's funhouse, might mandate
ten yards of distance from my body in public,

so I'm trying to drink in the closeness now,
tugging her by the hand through midday Manhattan,

business people slaloming the sidewalk
in rolled-up sleeves, taxi windows scrolled down.

Let's light a candle for Julia, Christine says matter-of-factly,
darting into a side door of St. Pat's. I expect

a couple tourists, two minutes max, but a service
is mid-bloom, hundreds in the pews. We slide in

to show Camilla how God works. A robed man
sings at a lectern, his voice—a butter knife

scraping fibula. Christine leafs through the prayer book.
My eyes go up and up to the chiseled ceiling.

The robed man's voice solves every crevice.
And I'm not religious and have no idea

what he's saying, but something happens
on this unnaturally hot autumn day. I don't have to hold

my face together anymore. This is a place
where you can let your face go.

And here it goes God, take Jamie's slumped body
from the sidewalk, blood seeping from his abdomen,

like whisky from a paper cup. Take my mother
and her wheelchair, and the six-year-old girl

behind her seventy-eight-year-old face. And take Julia's knee,
and my brother whose mind is elasticating

in two directions, like that Stretch Armstrong doll
we had as kids—how we pulled and pulled

to make him rip, but he wouldn't, so we jabbed
a screwdriver into his ribs, the purple Gelatin

oozing out, the purple Gelatin in my brother's brain,
but I don't have to be strong now. All of New York

felt like this in the first weeks after 9/11, people
sobbing in cafés, the fronts of fire stations

transformed into open-air flower shops, the clenched
expressions of the homeless suddenly apropos.

Invisible church singers belting out Ave Marias
on every corner, the smell of Christ's twin burnt bodies—

all you had to do was open your lips an inch
and let the mist into your lungs

and that was a homemade Eucharist. Bless the red-light
camera that took a little bite of my soul. Bless

the tooth dead in my mouth. Bless the bulb
dead in its socket. Bless my father

almost six months in the Earth. Bless the lungs
of the holy man singing. Bless this body

that has another thirty thousand miles left
according to the doctor, aka the mechanic of the flesh.

Bless the silence.　　Bless the hiss.　　Bless the punch.
Bless the kiss.　　Bless the lemon.　　Bless the lime.

Bless the fishbone in the throat of time.　　Bless
the fabric.　　Bless the rip.　　Bless the flame

swallowing the wick.　　The hour. The minute. The tick.

Arroyo Burro Beach

Nine-year-old boys pack orbs of wet sand
and chase each other up the shoreline.

Dogs, off-leash, churn after hurled tennis balls.
A trio of friends on a bedsheet chow pizza

with an uncorked bottle of supermarket wine.
A boogie boarder waits for the water to curve

so he can hop the wave, like a puck gliding
across an air hockey table. You drop your book,

smear on the no-burn lotion and lumber
into the surf. Kelp coils around your ankles

as you press in, up to your waist. You back-float
and let the ocean's cello hum sway you,

like you're in a liquid hammock, and all
the minor irritants, that were making the screws

in your spirit tighten, recede. The sun rubs
your belly with its warm yellow hand. You stand,

dip your paw beneath the surface and feel
a piece of seaweed. Tug it, like a green ponytail,

but it's rooted in the salt. You tug harder.
A fist in the sand yanks back. The fist

of a man recently dead. You wish you could
reach down and pull your father up

back into the shimmer. The beach is empty now,
the sun gone, but it left its nightlight on:

a sickle of reverberating moon.

California Night Sky

Mars is rising in the south, yellow and bright, rays shooting
off in five directions. *That starlight is a million years old,* says Mike.
I'll be wearing Kevlar underwear in a couple years,
says the traffic guard at the airport. *It was a 105 in the Valley today,*
says the newscaster. Carmen hands us a bowl of strawberries
and they explode like supernovas on the tongue. The Milky Way
is one drunk ass galaxy, how it looks like a jug
of constellation milk spilled on a glass table. *Andromeda
would be a cool name for a child,* says the wind. *That is one
nebulous babe,* said the astronomer in 964
just before he christened her. *But look at her galactic halo,*
said a rival star charter. The only things I've ever named
are five books and my daughter, Camilla Wren. *Mars
is bossing the night,* Rowan says, nine time zones away.
The president wants border crossings when you migrate
from Pacific to Mountain. Even for birds.
Rick Gates says he lied for Paul Manafort. *Tonight's my day off,*
says the moon. *How small you all look,* say the stars.

The Schadenfreude Channel

Hear ye, hear ye—in fifteen minutes
I'll be going live and squirming
in the dentist chair, the drill deep
in that mouth you've always wanted

to shut: face wrenched, neck
clenched, jagged nicks above the eyebrows,
spelling out *woe is yo* in cuneiform.
Listen close, and you'll hear me

whimpering over the drill's buzz saw.
So sit back and enjoy that Billy Idol sneer
wiped off my face's chalkboard
as the dentist smears maple syrup

on a Q-Tip and dabs it on the exposed
nerve of my left lower molar. Cut to a close-up
of my eyes, pupils thrashing like palm trees.
Trust me: it will taste like victory.

Tooth #19

My last endodontist slid assassin-like into the dentist office,
gripping a black bag with drills and reamers, hand files
and paste fillers—no small talk, zero banter—silenced
a tooth and jetted, never to be seen again. But this one

has a smile big enough to walk through. I confide:
"With a root canal some part of me is dying. It's one more step
on the road to oblivion." I consider a small funeral
in his waiting room. He injects Novocain into my gums,

waits, then drills. My fingers flash—tiny, beige bolts
of lightning. Fireworks of pain ricochet down my thighs.
He cocks his head at my lack of numbness. "Are you sure
it doesn't mean my molar is healthy and wants to live?"

"Your tooth is freaking out," he says.
"Maybe my tooth is like a person who fell off a boat
and is frantically waving its hands at us, saying, *save me*,
and you're essentially pushing it under the surface,

telling it to drown." "I wouldn't think of it like that.
Your tooth wants to die, and I'm helping it," he says,
pumping a double dose of Novocain. But still a blast of air
feels like a wrecking ball pulverizing the nerve.

He takes off his blue mask. "I can't get you numb."
But I hear, *I can't get it up.* "This has never happened
to me before," he says. But I think about that drunken night
sophomore year. "No wonder you were such a drug addict,"

my pal Alex says. I ask Sloane to read Jewish scripture
at my follow-up. I say the French call an orgasm

the little death. "You do a lot of that in your twenties,"
she says, "but after fifty it's all tumors and teeth."

We're gathered here today to say good-bye to tooth number 19,
a lower molar with two roots, who chewed with abandon
through licorice and Skittles, taffy and candy corn.
19 didn't complain. He did the work that was in front of him.

His crime: he wanted to go down with the ship,
but in the end was disposed of like a stowaway. Not even the dignity
of waltzing the plank. No, he was tossed overboard,
his long roots clawing at the lip.

The Pain

The pain started out small at first:
a toddler tracking sand over the gash.

Soon enough the pain was in middle school,
wearing headphones everywhere, surly

at the kitchen table, shoving its fingers
into the wound as you slept. And poof—

the pain is old enough to drive, pressing
its boot down on the accelerator, leaving

skid marks in the lesion, your whole head
pulsating like a nightclub, speakers blaring

mixtapes of chainsaws and dentist drills,
and still the pain is growing, asking you

to co-sign the lease of its first apartment
with your finger dipped in blood.

Amsterdam

You prowl the streets of Amsterdam
so high that the bicycle wheels seem to spin
through the air like metallic constellations,
and there's such a disconnect
between how lit you are and how
the Dutch are just living their lives,
pedaling home from work, and the sky
is so swirly you think Van Gogh
and you run your hand along the railing
overlooking a canal. The sun packs up
its light and pulls it away
like a child dragging a yellow towel
from the beach, and then the red lights
flicker in the multiplying darkness,
but instead of blonde Serbians
in face paint and translucent negligees,
men in black robes with stiff white collars
stand solemnly, and instead of pin-eyed
middle-aged tourists and college boys
drifting in, it's ten-year-old kids
entering the glass cages, fed
to the beast of the lord. And you thank
your cross-eyed stars you were raised
agnostic. You remember going
with your buddy Drew, an altar boy,
after Saturday sleepovers, and standing in line
for the man, who dipped his digits in
the finger bowl so you could open your mouth
wide and let him place the body of Christ
on the gurney of your tongue.

Eighth Grade

The guy you've been crushing on all year
in math class just leaned in for a kiss. The only problem:
you left the dentist an hour ago, and your mouth
is as numb as a 1970s housewife. His tongue
could be methodically painting your gums
for all you know. Hopefully he won't tell everyone
you're a bad kisser. Ah, the joys of middle school.
The bio teacher with the Velcro moustache.
The lunch lady with her wooden spoon.
How long is a kiss even supposed to last for?
His lips feel as far away as a stereo
playing in a neighbor's backyard.
Is your tongue even moving? *Wait right here*, you say,
and run down the stairs of Lily Pruitt's house
and into the backyard, where the sun
is throwing handfuls of yellow rice at your feet.

The Used Bookstore of Your Dreams

You walk into a used bookstore
and the entire poetry section
is filled with signed books of yours.
Dear Becky, your smile cuts through me
like a knife through cheesecake. You tell yourself
she was probably downsizing
and the fact that she sold this,
for less than a dollar, is not a testament
to the bushel of nights you spent together
sucking light from the moon.
Dear Lou, friends since the womb,
then a man in a white bodysuit enters
with a vacuum. He takes your first book
and sucks all the words off each page.
Vacuums off the blurb,
that always felt a little over the top,
and then sucks off the cover art
that you were so excited about.
Then he swallows all the letters
of your name, except for the *y*,
and throws the book down and grabs
another. You lunge and he slurps up
your left hand, your whole arm
into the machine. The louder
you scream, the more he erases
until the only thing left
is your right hand. He places
a pen in your palm and closes
your fingers around the stem
and whispers, *let's see you*
write your way out of this one, champ.

Hymens Are Stronger than Trampolines

When she told me that my ego was *as delicate
as a porcelain bull*, it really got my dander up,
which is to say the dandruff on my head
stood and threw its tiny white hands

into the air. When she added that *rage
is an erection for the impotent*, a Bunsen burner
in my chest ignited and the pot of blood
that feeds my veins started to boil.

When she continued, *why don't you
go eat some porno vitamins and transform
your penis into a hood ornament
for the souped-up Porsche of your psychosis,*

the sky turned as red as my mother's lipstick
on a Friday night. *You have more potholes
in your brain than the Brooklyn Queens Expressway.
Go meet your guy friends at the bar and have one*

*of your misogyny training sessions, I mean
boys' nights out?* And my mouth was as empty
as a public pool after a lightning bolt
signs its name across the sky.

Genital Odometers

We need odometers on genitals
so we know what we're getting into,
said a man. Of course, he's the one
whose loins turned out to be a '79 Pinto
with a busted carburetor and grease stains
on the pleather seats. *Your dick is so limp*
you need Viagra just to get pee shy
at the public urinal, yelled the cool girls
out the window of their Volvo, or at least
that's what T. S. Eliot said. Duchamp
changed urinals forever. After him
urinals started getting all artsy-fartsy
and men guzzled glow-in-the-dark Gatorade
so they could make Etch-A-Sketch pee art.
My buddy Joan has a t-shirt that says: *The women cum*
and go, talking shit about Michelangelo. In college
my friend drank from a bidet like a water fountain.
Are you trying to be scandalous? my wife says,
reading the first draft of this, but she doesn't know
what it's like to be fourteen years old
at the urinal, the football team
gathered round, chanting *art, art, art,*
as you squeeze your paint brush and try
to take one for the team, their jockstraps
swinging overhead like the lassoes of puberty,
or those wicked haloes painted by Fra Angelico.

The Narcoleptic's Marathon

The hetero married version of a 69 is: she does the dishes
while he folds the laundry. The sadomasochistic version

of a hand job involves sandpaper gloves. My body
is an old house; you fix one thing and something

else breaks. Today at the beach, a dolphin
sucked the wedding ring right off someone's finger.

The decay is down to your gums, said the dentist.
This cabinet will have to come out. The narcoleptic's

marathon involves twenty-six beds and strategically placed
alarm clock stations. In Sweden, there is a little jar

for you to spit your dreams into, in the bathroom
when you wake up. In France, married couples

must have sex in front of beginners once a year.
Encular nuit. I never liked that molar anyway.

The hole in my mouth where tooth number eighteen was
feels like a burnt-out bedroom. When I was twenty,

this girl literally set my futon on fire, and the firemen
chucked my stuff from the kicked-out dorm window.

When I was twenty-one, a different classmate
metaphorically set my bed on fire and left claw marks

on my vertebrae, and we role-played a couple firemen
squirting us with water pistols. She had great teeth

and now she has a couple kids and a wedding ring
the size of a strobe light. When I see her

at our fiftieth reunion, I'll whisper in her flower petal ear:
honey is the only food that never goes bad.

Creation Myth

You're in a dentist office—plastic flowers
on the sill. The dentist is showing you close-ups
of the bombed-out factory
that is your brother's mouth. Fourteen years
without a check-up will do that to you.
Let's get some muzak up in this motherfucker,
you want to yell, but instead bite your lip.
Outside the sky looks like it's been punched
in the face. It's the rainiest July in our lifetimes.
He told me he hasn't brushed in months,
the dentist said in the hallway. *I really like
when my patients are honest with me.*

An hour later we're at my dad's apartment,
turning the keys in. Last year, the old man
went over Niagara Falls in a giant Diet Coke can,
the cords from his oxygen tank flailing in the wind,
like the electric hair of science.
Fifty years before that he was pushing
his Protestant telescope into our mother's night sky
and belting out the names of constellations:
Andromeda, Jonathan, Libra,
and my mother screamed out: *yes,
yes, let's name him Jonathan.*

And thus, my six-foot-tall brother
with broomsticks for limbs
clacked and clacked into being.

November

The News

It's the first day of November.
The sky is a white tarp
with a small rip in the fabric,
where the yellow trickles through.
In the summer, the Eiffel Tower
can be up to six inches taller.
That's a seasonal boner,
cracks the seventh-grade boy
forever treading water
in my torrent of consciousness;
in reality it's just thermal
expansion. All across America
kids are stockpiling candy bars
under their beds. Dentists
are licking their chops
at all those future cavities. Trees
are halting the production of chlorophyll,
and the leaves are starting to die,
which we humans love.
Imagine a person suffocating
and a couple oak trees admiring
the shade of blueish pale in the cheeks.
Yes, the temperature climbed
the thermometer's spiral staircase
into the sixties today, and I'm fine
in a t-shirt. But it's still time
to pack away my shorts
until April. Winter is coming
to my wardrobe, to my skin,
my hairline, my lungs. *Winter
is going to cum on your face,*
howls my inner seventh grader,

who doesn't seem to realize
that when I belly flop into eternity,
him and his tighty whities
are flopping too.

The Yard Is Covered with Yellow Leaves

The yard is covered with yellow leaves, tiny hands
waving good-bye. *But who are they waving good-bye to?*
asks my eight-year-old niece. *Could it be the branches,*
I ask. *Or the tree itself? The oak who fed them water
from its roots? Or perhaps they're waving to us—*
Wait a second, my niece interrupts.
Who do you think you are? Walt Whitman?
She's right. Truth is: the leaves are debris
that I will rake into a trash bag tomorrow
in forty-degree weather. Today I am too busy
painting a first coat on the new shed
we keep our bikes in. Truth is: I've barely hiked
at all this autumn, so to romanticize seasonal imagery
borders on the dishonest. Admiring
the foliage while driving to work is not the same.
Next autumn, I'll walk more, ride my bike more,
focus on the leaves, tiny green stopwatches
that turn yellow and red, the message the same
in every language: *time is passing, slow down,*
observe, breathe, another season in the can.
You're going to die, motherfucker, the leaves scream,
but the night is descending like a giant spider,
and I have to get on a second coat of paint,
as if a second coat could save me.

Tonight's Lecture: What Not To Do When Painting

One: Don't Paint in the Dark. You might think the moon
is a nightlight, but, when the sun drops behind the tree-line
like a tennis ball on fire, it's time to wrap things up,
regardless of what artificial deadlines you've booby-trapped
your brain with. Two: Don't Wear Your Birthday Fleece
and get it all polka-dotted with *Pismo Dunes* and then
have to spray Windex all over the *Pismo* blobs and the next day
wear it inside out and inhale all the ammonia in the fabric
and later wonder why you feel dizzy. Three: Don't Hold the Roller
in One Hand and the Brush in the Other. Inevitably
you'll splatter an archipelago onto your gray sweats
and whatever pleasure you're deriving from this endeavor
will evaporate and be replaced with molecules of regret.
Four: Speaking of Pleasure, remember
what your dead father said: "when you were a toddler,
we'd just bought the house on Spruce Street,
and I'd go into your room after work, while you slept,
and I had this flashlight. And I'd paint a little bit
each night. And your mother came up to me after
and said, *you really get some weird joy out of doing that,
don't you?* And that's when I knew I was in this all alone."
Five: Even If You're Painting by Yourself
in forty-degree weather, try not to be in this all alone.

Biophilia

My love, after our meal of foraged parsnips
and untamed carrots, I will lather your arms

in Gorilla Glue and smear fallen birch leaves
on your limbs. I've covered the bed in spruce needles

and dabbed pine resin on my nipples. That sound
you hear in the background is the mating call of a peacock

layered over a trip-hop beat, based on the rhythmic pounding
of ocean mating with rock. The windows are open wide.

The pillows are filled with clumps of Whitman's beard.
My love, your eyes are lit matches frozen in amber,

and your hair is a biodegradable cup of Pepsi
hurled from an electric car.

Wolf Energy

Some people have wolf energy—visible
either in the jaw or the lean, rising shoulders,
a gait radiating speed. Other people
have rabbit energy. If you were sleeping
and they bit your neck, it might strike you
as ticklish. Others have bear energy—oversized,
cuddly, but liable to snarl and swipe your face
with a paw. Cat energy is first cousins
with skunk energy. My wife says my face
looks like a shark's, but squirrel teeth
line my gums. If I chomp you,
you won't lose an arm. My half-brother
is an owl that flew into the woods
and never came back. My one brother
is half-rhino and half-blowtorch.
My other brother is a puddle of water
evaporating in a cave. Each day
I check to make sure he's still there.

A Man Walks into a Bar

A man walks into a bar. It's not just any man.
It's your father, back from the dead, carrying souvenirs
from the underworld in a plastic bag. A cheap t-shirt
with a silhouette of Hades's face. A deck of trick cards
with Lazarus as the joker. Your father's wearing a Panama hat
and a denim vest. He looks twenty years younger. No more
oxygen tank slung over his shoulder like a rocket launcher.
Bombay and tonic, he says to the female bartender, her dark hair
pulled back in a bun. *Nice to see you, Walt*, she says,
Her voice is a peppermint lozenge dissolving in your ear.
It's your mother, the woman he crashed and burned with
thirty-three years ago. This is too much, you think,
and go outside, where your brothers are giddy preteens
with white athletic socks up to their knees. Your hair
grows back faster than a Chia Pet. The word *baldness*
is erased from the dictionary. *Boys, time for dinner*,
your mom says. This is the happy childhood we never had
you're tempted to say, but then that home-cooked
mac and cheese hits your nose, and the hostility
evaporates from your face. The bar has been replaced
with a clean dining room and a mother whose eyes
are not hazel coins vanishing into a lake.

Parking Lot Jesus

Why is that grown man jumping up and down in the parking lot
yelling *fuck*? It's the Friday after Thanksgiving. The air cold enough

to freeze your saliva if you spat into a bowl. The moon, pregnant
with possibility, rubs its round belly in the sky, wonders

what sort of mayhem it will give birth to. The man has just stacked
a dozen shopping bags from Trader Joe's on top of suitcases

and food bags etc., and sank into the bucket seat of his new electric car.
The man is just small enough to feel a sense of accomplishment

at making it all fit, when his wife says "what about a beverage"
to go with the popcorn puffs and peanut butter cups he's set aside

to eat in the car. Look inside the man's body and you will see
the pulleys tighten his neck from within. See the nail holes

in his palm, the thorns in his buzz cut, yanking out grocery bags
and *whoosh*—the organic blueberries hit the ground and explode

from their clear plastic container and rush across the asphalt,
a purplish-blue referendum on the man's soul. Hence

his pogoing into the air several times, like an exclamation point
gone rogue. The man crouches and scoops the runaway fruits.

Let's examine the roots of the tantrum: a hundred miles
and thirteen hours earlier, his brother's place, the secondhand smoke

so thick his eyes watered, the bathtub with no shower curtain,
the seven trash bags of laundry. The man utterly helpless

to influence the flight of birds in the brother's head. This absence
of power is where the tantrum started, but you would not know this

if you were sitting in your car and watching the man yell *fuck*
and jump up and down in a Trader Joe's parking lot

over spilled blueberries, the Friday night after Thanksgiving.

Personalized Russian Dolls

Twenty-two hours later, and you're stepping off
a plane and into a clearing. A corpse

is lying on the ground. It's the person you used to be.
Think about how much money you'd make,

marketing personalized Russian dolls
with five different wooden incarnations

of a person's self. You as a balding middle-aged man
in a plaid shirt and trousers. You in a red tank top

and combat boots howling into a tulip.
You with scraggly dreads and a solar eclipse

reflected in your shimmering eyes. You in white sneakers,
running from the cops, your right hand covered

in red spray paint, like you dipped your fist
in a burgundy cookie jar. You as a diabolically smiling

eight-year-old, your fingers a pack of matches
ready to set the world on fire, no, your fingers

ten scissor blades ready to give the world
a haircut. There now, ease into the chair.

Inside that last little worry doll is a frozen droplet
of your father's miracle juice, the pearl-colored race car

that whisked you into the parking garage
of your mother's womb.

It's been November for several months now

My daughter just turned twelve. New stuff is happening
inside her body. A new president is voted into office
every few hours. The statues of last year
have been torn down. One minute she's punching me
in the stomach, and the next we're passing
a grapefruit-sized foam ball, small enough
that she can catch and grip it with one hand.
Talk flows when we toss the ball.
The lines of communication open
both literally and figuratively. And I'm not saying
having a daughter prance through puberty's minefield
is a cakewalk, but there are stretches like this,
her right arm extended over her burnt umber strands,
snatching the ball, flicking it back,
spilling the tea from school, unpacking the talk
on vaping we attended together, and for a few minutes
my opinion means something, and we're turning
off the lamp, and I'm reading *The Hate U Give*
with a flashlight, and I want this moment
to elongate, as she sinks evenly into sleep,
in this room, where I peeled off the old wallpaper
with a knife just after she was born.

2050

Suppose I said 2050. What do you mean?
Would you take 2050? What am I selling?
The year. Would you take it,
if I put it on the table? That's eighty-three.
Another thirty-two years of watching
the trees slip out of their green
dresses and asking: will you
still love me when I'm old and frail?

Each year trees get born again
and go through adolescence.
Each year they're robust and strapping.
Each year they have their youth
ripped from their hands, gripping their leaves
like a gambler clutching poker chips.
Each year they sag through middle age.

Anyway, this is about 2050: flying cars,
colleges offering degrees in spontaneity,
water pills—an entire gallon in a single drop,
scientists struggling to force stadium-sized
tranquilizers down the schizophrenic throat
of Mother Nature. Half the planet dripping
with nuclear waste. And me eighty-three,

needing a cane to reach the sink. Knees
shot. Lungs moth-eaten. My penis:
a dangling modifier without a sentence.
Squinting. Squawking *What?!*
Catching my breath on staircases. Slipping
my teeth in a jar each night. My daughter
forty-four. Yes, my friend, I will take it.

The Hour the Beards of the Dead Get Their Growth

Is that African mask eyeing me?
Do those sharpened pencils
poking up from the block of wood
want to thrust into the pulp

of my caramel irises? It's three a.m.
all the lies I've told in my lifetime
are being sorted into piles.
The lawn mower battery

charger keeps blinking red
to green. I wish my father
was in this room, but not the person
he was alive: always flashing

conflicting lights, but a better
version, who could listen.
My stomach protrudes
over the rim of my pajamas.

Who eats chili on a hamburger bun
with ketchup after two a.m.?
What I miss for my father
is not me and him. We were goats

on a hillside; it's sitting in the dark
watching his granddaughter
pirouette across hardwood.
Maybe the blinking light is for him.

Maybe he doesn't know
whether to stay or go. No,

that's stupid—he left two years ago.
I saw him with my own eyes

lift over the Atlantic
leaving a vapor trail
like a piece of toilet paper
hanging from his boxers.

Forest Walk by the Hudson

58° mid-March, the warmth almost disorienting
after last week's polar vortex. Taking stock

of winter's wreckage. Trees tipped flat, roots
reaching out like the hands of beggars.

I wish I felt connected to the river, or the nubs
of plants plotting under the dirt's surface,

or even the mud that looks shiny
in the four o'clock sun, or the ice clumps,

but my object correlative here is the toppled trees.
Yet I'm still standing. How much decay

is in my soil? How much wind until my roots
unravel? The Hudson barely ripples. The weather app

predicted a hard breeze, but I don't feel it. November snow
still carpets Storm King mountain. A train

howls south. A cannon coughs hard at the army base.
I step from the forest and feel the wind. I was protected

in an inlet and didn't realize it. The story of my life.
Maybe I do feel connected to the river. The way it has fish

under the surface that we can't see: bass, flounder,
sturgeon. The way it's been abused

and pumped with mercury and lead, not dissimilar
to all the formaldehyde and paint thinner I flooded

my bloodstream with. I'm coming up on twenty-five years
with no drugs. Bruised, but still flowing. Sometimes

canoes go across my surface. Sometimes people
spit into me. There are boots on the bottom of me

with human feet inside. But I keep flowing. I smooth
over the rocks and polish the bones of my dead.

Wooden Bench

I was sitting on a wooden bench
when six men wheeled her on a gurney right past me,

except she was inside a wooden box
and the lid was closed. She was on her way

to becoming a skeleton. My father
is definitely a skeleton at this point.

Death is confusing. Is my father the bones
that sit inside a box on a hillside

in Odessa, Delaware? Or is he on the other side
of that keyhole in my mind that I talk into sometimes?

Can he be in two places at once? Am I allowed
to make it up, the way 12-step programs tell you

you can make up God. God can be a ribbon
on the door, a nail in the wall.

A nail in the coffin. It's 4:59 a.m. The sky
a deep ocean blue. The birds going nuts

in the trees. Do birds dream?
My daughter likes to tell me her dreams,

especially when I do something bad.
In an hour, she'll get up for school.

It's exactly mid-May and half the trees on this street
don't have any leaves. Do I miss my father?

In his presence, my head would start to throb
like a blister and I'd take naps in random places

to make the throbbing stop. We were close
when I was a child, and he wasn't lying when he said

he was my history book. The birds are whistling
but they are not whistling for me.

Vampire Schedule

For the past few weeks
I've been on this vampire schedule.

The morning birds in the trees singing me
a bed time story. But I'm not allergic

to sunlight. A few weeks ago
I was on a werewolf schedule.

What's tough about being a werewolf
is the transformation: an earthquake of fur

sprouting from your follicles. A vampire
just sleeps inside a coffin.

The dilemma of being a vampire
is when you need blood.

But you don't transform or anything.
And it's greatly exaggerated

how much blood a vampire
actually needs to survive.

And it doesn't have to be all human.
Frankenstein schedules suck,

feeling like an art piece
in someone else's studio. Cocaine

used to turn me into a cyclops
and all I could see with my one eye

was more coke. Yesterday
I saw three high-flying birds

over the Hudson, and right away
I thought *three-eyed raven.*

The vampire schedule is tough
when you live with regular humans,

your overlap of experience
shrinks. The weird thing is

I don't even like the taste of blood.
but I like being up all night,

holding pieces of tissue
over the mouths of the people sleeping

and see the tissue lift into the air
like a flying carpet.

Imagine you're in a tall cave, and there's a bird flying,
and you cannot see the bird, and you cannot hear the bird,
but you can feel the echo of its wings, and its tiny breeze
going through your hair slow, not exactly like a comb,
maybe like someone's fingers, someone you used to know.
That's all we have now. The physical echo of his fingers.
And somewhere the bird is flying higher and higher
and leaving the cave, right through the mountain and now
a ray of light is coming in, and now the stone is opening,
and now it's filled with light and we see the blue sky
and the bird is gone.

acknowledgments

The following poems first appeared in these journals:

American Poetry Review: "Gigantic"; *Bat City Review*: "Set Design Notes for a Seizure"; *Bennington Review*: "The Bottom of My Hourglass," "My Adobe Bouquet," "Arroyo Burro Beach," and "Amsterdam"; *Boatt*: "Creation Myth" and "Destruction Myth"; *Columbia Magazine:* "The Imperial Diet"; *Poetry Daily*: "Jonathan"; *Prairie Schooner*: "The Church of Michael Jordan"; *Southampton Review*: "Midlife Chrysler," "Pass the Gravy," and "Bio from a Parallel World."

"The Church of Michael Jordan" was reprinted on Poets.org and in the anthology *A Body of Athletics*, edited by Natalie Diaz.

"Bio from a Parallel World" was reprinted in *Best American Poetry 2019*, edited by Major Jackson.

"The Hour the Beards of the Dead Get Their Growth" gets its title from a W. S. Merwin poem.

Thanks to Christine Caballero, Kendra DeColo, Amy Gerstler, and Ivy Meeropol for reading earlier versions of this book, and to Julia Edwards for shepherding it to the finish line.

Thanks to Ed Ochester and the people at Pitt Press for their excellent work.

Thanks to Jasmin Siddiqui (also known as Hera from the German-based street art duo Herakut) for the painting on the cover.